WELCOME TO BLOODY DIFFICULT BRITAIN

FIRST PUBLISHED IN THE UNITED KINGDOM
IN 2017 BY

PORTICO
43 GREAT ORMOND STREET
LONDON
WC1N 3HZ

AN IMPRINT OF PAVILION BOOKS COMPANY LTD

ISBN 9781911042952

A CIP CATALOGUE RECORD FOR THIS BOOK IS
AVAILABLE FROM THE BRITISH LIBRARY.

10 9 8 7 6 5 4 3 2 1 ...

PRINTED AND BOUND BY CPI GROUP (UK) LTD CHATHAM

DESIGNED AND ILLUSTRATED BY RORY LOWE.

THIS BOOK CAN BE ORDERED DIRECT FROM THE
PUBLISHER AT WWW.PAVILIONBOOKS.COM

WELCOME TO BLOODY DIFFICULT BRITAIN

A SELF-HELP GUIDE TO SURVIVING THE UK'S IDENTITY CRISIS, DIVORCE FROM THE EU, AND WESTMINSTER'S TOTAL POLITICAL BREAKDOWN

THERESA MEH

TAKE A MORE CAREFREE APPROACH
TO LIFE.

BRAINERCISE

GIVE YOURSELF A MENTAL
WORKOUT WITH THESE POLITICIAN -
BASED ANAGRAMS.

EVOG SI A WEALES

YAM ASH ON PORTPUS

NORBCY SI A MAM JAKER

AINI NUDNAC THIMS TEAS SABIEB

NORIS SI A BOB

EUROSTAR WARS

EPISODE IV – NOT A HOPE

ESCAPE INTO AN EXCITING WORLD OF
SCI-FI ADVENTURE. READ THE
FOLLOWING PLOT SET-UP AND THEN
WRITE AN ENDING.

IN A GALAXY FAR, FAR AWAY, THE EVIL
GALACTIC UNION IS CONTINUING TALKS
WITH THE PLUCKY REBEL PLANET
BRITOOINE. GOVERNED BY THE
STRUGGLING PRINCESS MAYA,
BRITOOINE IS A WORLD IN CONFLICT.

SICK OF THE EVIL UNION'S ATTEMPTS TO STANDARDISE PORK PRODUCTS, PLACE RESTRICTIONS ON SPACE FISHING ZONES, AND ALLOW FREEDOM OF MOVEMENT, THE PEOPLE (52% OF THEM, AT LEAST) HAVE REBELLED AND ORDERED THE GOVERNMENT TO LEAVE THE EVIL UNION.

PANICKED, CONFUSED, AND TOTALLY INEFFECTUAL, PRINCESS MAYA HAS ORDERED HER TOP NEGOTIATORS BORIS ZIPWIREHANGER AND OFFICIOUS TORYBOT, DAVID D4V15 TO LEAD THE DELEGATION TO BEGIN THE SENSITIVE AND FRAGILE EXIT NEGOTIATIONS. BUT ARE THEY HEADING FOR AN AMBUSH?

BRITAIN'S NEXT TOP
PRIME MINISTER

DISILLUSIONED WITH THE UK'S
CURRENT LEADERSHIP? WHY NOT
IMAGINE SOMEONE BETTER AS PM?

GORDON THE
GOPHER

VICTOR
MELDREW

MARY BERRY

RELEASE THE PRESSURE

COPE WITH THE PRESSURE OF BEING BRITISH.

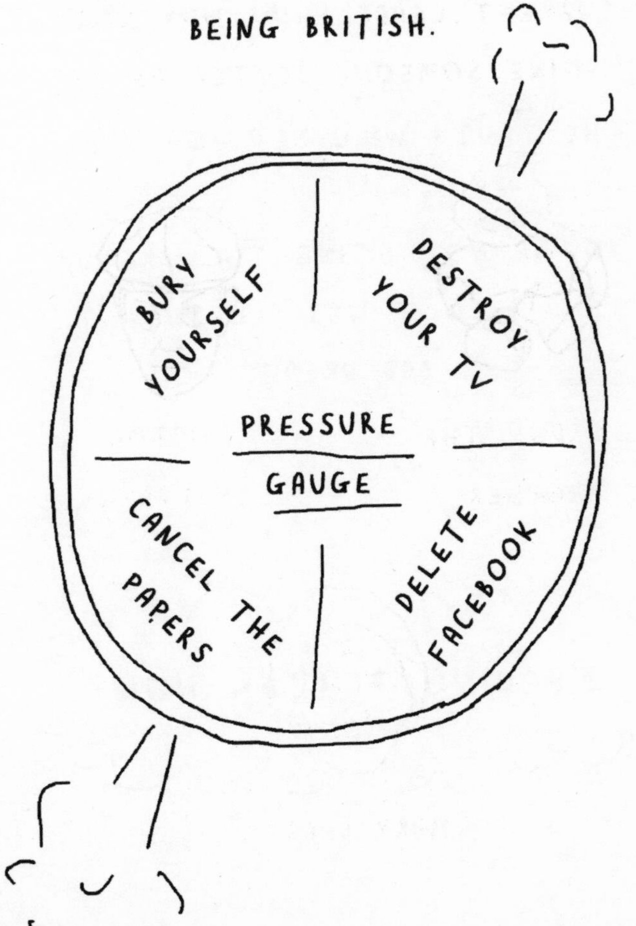

FACE FACTS

THE TRUTH WILL SET YOU FREE.

YOU'RE NOT GOING TO WAKE UP
AND FIND IT WAS ALL JUST A
BAD DREAM.

FEELING BETTER NOW?

DESIGN FOR LIFE

IMAGINE YOU'RE A TOP FASHION
DESIGNER. DESIGN A GARMENT TO
HELP FUEL YOUR POSITIVITY AND
LIFT YOUR SPIRITS.

THE BASEBALL CAP OF
UNFATHOMABLE POPULARITY

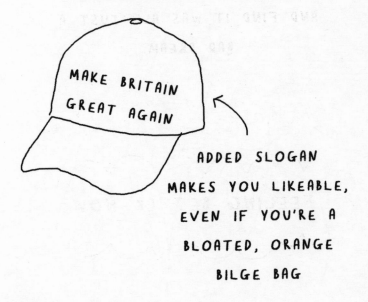

MAKE BRITAIN
GREAT AGAIN

ADDED SLOGAN
MAKES YOU LIKEABLE,
EVEN IF YOU'RE A
BLOATED, ORANGE
BILGE BAG

RAYS OF HOPE

1. MEARS

2. WINSTONE

3. DAVIES

4. REARDON

5. PARLOUR

6. ALAN AND LORD CHARLES

CORBYN CONFESSION CORNER

CONFESS YOUR SINS AND PURGE YOUR SOUL.

RU E L

BRITANNIA

DVD DETOX

ESCAPE THE HARSH REALITIES OF
BRITISH POLITICS BY RELAXING IN
FRONT OF YOUR FAVOURITE DVD.

THE JEREMY HUNT FOR RED OCTOBER

LAST TANGO IN BORIS

BREXIT AT TIFFANY'S

FIFTY SHADES OF GRAYLING

FARAGE – INTERNATIONAL
PERSON OF INTEREST

TRY TO BE OPEN-MINDED AND TAKE OTHERS' INTERESTS INTO ACCOUNT.

BLAH, BLAH, BLAH. DID I EVER TELL YOU ABOUT THE TIME I WENT SHORE FISHING IN CLACTON? BLAH, BLAH, BLAH...

ZZZZZ

DISTRACTION ACTIONS

DISTRACT YOURSELF FROM YOUR
WORRIES ABOUT THE UK BY
WORRYING ABOUT SOMETHING
MUCH WORSE:

1. AN ASTEROID ENDS ALL LIFE
   ON THE PLANET

2. A SPANISH FLU OUTBREAK
   WIPES OUT MILLIONS

3. THE PRICE OF BEER GOES UP

ACERBIC UNICORN

YOU ARE ZORN, A PROUD AND
MAGICAL UNICORN WARRIOR. USE
YOUR POWERS TO HUNT DOWN
POLITICIANS AND MAKE THEM REPENT
BY WITTILY RE-NAMING THEM.

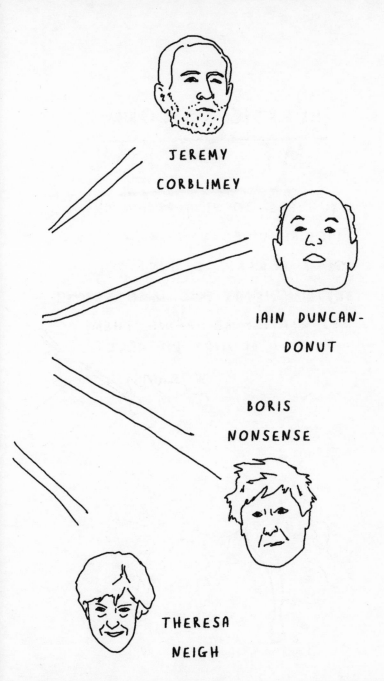

JEREMY
CORBLIMEY

IAIN DUNCAN-
DONUT

BORIS
NONSENSE

THERESA
NEIGH

MT -> TM

"BRITAIN NEEDS ~~AN~~ ~~IRON~~ ~~LADY!~~"
          V
              BLOODY DIFFICULT
                  WOMAN

JC NUGGETS

WITH JEREMY'S SECOND COMING HE
SEEMS TO HAVE MORE WISDOM THAN
EVER. RECEIVE HIS NUGGETS AND
FEED OFF THEM.

HORSES CAN SLEEP
BOTH STANDING UP
AND LYING DOWN.

NO ACT OF
KINDNESS,
HOWEVER SMALL,
IS EVER WASTED

GRIME EMERGED FROM
LONDON'S EAST END IN
THE EARLY 2000'S. IN
2003 DIZZEE RASCAL'S
'BOY IN DA CORNER' WON
THE MERCURY MUSIC
PRIZE. GRIME HAD ARRIVED!

EU
LOOK. CAN WE JUST HAVE A GROWN-UP CONVERSATION ABOUT THIS BREAK-UP?
UK
I'M IN A BAD PLACE AT THE MOMENT. I'M ALL OVER THE SHOP.
EU
BUT WHAT ABOUT CUSTODY? SCOTLAND WANTS TO COME WITH ME.
UK
WHATEVER. JUST LET ME KEEP LITTLE GIBRALTAR. I DON'T WANT YOU RUINING HER TOO!
EU
YOU'RE BEING CHILDISH.
UK
I'M NOT BEING CHILDISH. YOU'RE CHILDISH. I JUST DON'T LOVE YOU ANY MORE. GET OVER IT.
EU
I'M TRYING TO HELP YOU. YOU NEED HELP.
UK
NO. YOU'RE TRYING TO TELL ME WHAT TO DO. LIKE YOU ALWAYS DO. JUST LEAVE ME ALONE.

IMAGI-NATION

TRY TO IMAGINE A BRITAIN THAT IS
UNITED AND AT ONE.
IMAGINE GREAT WEATHER, BEAUTIFUL
SCENERY AND A PROGRESSIVE
POLITICAL ENVIRONMENT.

OR GIVE UP DAYDREAMING AND
MOVE TO CANADA.

RETENTIVE RELEASE

EMBRACE YOUR INNER PEDANT BY
WIPING ALL THE TOOTHPASTE
OFF THIS MESSY TUBE'S NOZZLE.

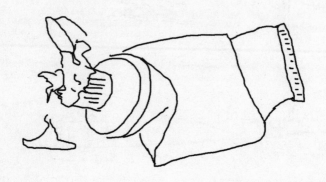

AUSTERITY ANGEL

IT'S GOOD TO PURGE YOURSELF OF
ANY UNNECESSARY TREATS IN LIFE.
HERE IS A LIST OF LUXURIES -
SEE WHICH YOU CAN DO WITHOUT?

CHOCOLATE

THE
FIRE BRIGADE

WINE

FISH & CHIPS

TELEVISION

THE GYM

NURSES

BOVRIL

ADEQUATELY FUNDED
LOCAL COUNCILS

CAN YOU THINK OF ANY MORE?

THERESA MAY'S
CARPENTRY CORNER

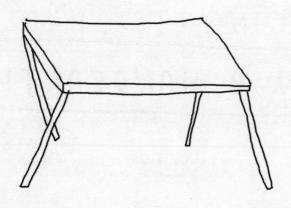

A STRONG AND STABLE TABLE.

WE ARE ALL GOING TO HELL IN A HANDCART!

LAUGHTER THERAPY

HERE COMES BOJO THE CLOWN.
WHAT'S HE DOING NOW?

IS HE USING HIS FUNNY
MADE-UP WORDS AGAIN?

LEARN TO BE

PATRIOTIC AGAIN

HAVE A GOOD OLD SING-SONG
AROUND THE CAMP FIRE.

'WE'LL MEET AGAIN, DON'T KNOW
WHERE, DON'T KNOW WHEN.'

(BUT LET'S FACE IT, IT WILL
PROBABLY BE IN THE DOLE QUEUE.)

HAMMOND HOUSE

OF HORROR

 TO BE AFRAID HELPS US TO FACE UP TO THE HARD KNOCKS LIFE THROWS AT US.

INTRODUCING:

THE TONY BLAIR WITCH PROJECT

BRITISH BALL

YOU HAVE A SHINY, BOUNCY BALL.
TOSS IT INTO THE ROAD AND
WITH EACH BOUNCE WAVE GOODBYE
TO AN UNWANTED ASPECT OF
YOUR NATIONAL IDENTITY.

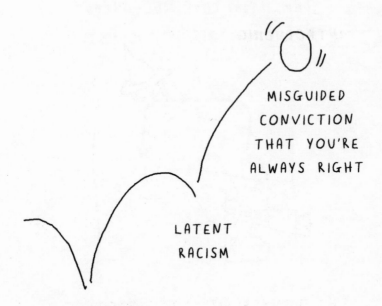

MISGUIDED
CONVICTION
THAT YOU'RE
ALWAYS RIGHT

LATENT
RACISM

POOR DECISION-
MAKING RE BREXIT

THERESA MAY SCHOOL

OF MOTORING

PUT YOURSELF IN LIFE'S
DRIVING SEAT.

THERE'S AN UNPOPULAR
'DEMENTIA TAX' BILL AHEAD.
PERFORM THIS MANOEUVRE:

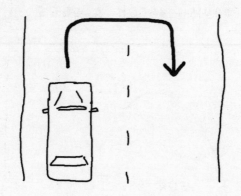

THE U TURN

THE BREXIT CAFE

EAT YOURSELF HEALTHY.

I. THE BREXIT BREAKFAST

TODAY'S SPECIALS

~~FRENCH CROISSANTS~~

~~DANISH BACON & EGGS~~

~~ITALIAN ESPRESSO~~

TOAST

~~HOPE~~

~~BON APPETIT~~

ENJOY YOUR MEAL!

POLITICAL PARTY TIME

IT'S YOUR PARTY. RE-SHUFFLE
YOUR SHADOW CABINET WITH A
GAME OF MUSICAL CHAIRS.

LANGUAGE, TIMOTHY!

FAKE NEWS

FED UP WITH DEPRESSING HEADLINES?
WHY NOT MAKE UP SOME FAKE ONES
TO CHEER YOURSELF UP?

STIFF UPPER LIP

KEEP CALM AND CARRY ON -
TEST YOUR ANGER CONTROL WITH
THIS IMAGE.

WHERE'S VLAD?

TEST YOUR POWERS OF
OBSERVATION.

ANSWER - HE'S BEHIND
THE HEADLINES.

ZONAL HAPPINESS

CREATE SAFE SPACES AROUND YOUR
HOME WHERE YOU CAN BE FREE
FROM STRESS AND ANXIETY.

TURN YOUR SHED INTO A
NO-GOVE ZONE.

THERESA MEH

TAKE A MORE CAREFREE APPROACH
TO LIFE.

BRITAIN'S NEXT TOP
PRIME MINISTER

DISILLUSIONED WITH THE UK'S
CURRENT LEADERSHIP? WHY NOT
IMAGINE SOMEONE BETTER AS PM?

SOOTY

SCARLETT
FROM
GOGGLEBOX

GRAND MOFF
TARKIN

EUROSTAR WARS

EPISODE V – THE UNION

STRIKES BACK

ESCAPE INTO AN EXCITING WORLD OF
SCI-FI ADVENTURE. READ THE
FOLLOWING PLOT SET-UP AND THEN
WRITE AN ENDING.

IN A GALAXY FAR, FAR AWAY,
PRINCESS MAYA, THE MARGINALLY
ELECTED LEADER OF REBEL PLANET
BRITOOINE, IS STILL TRYING TO
LEAVE BEHIND THE WRATH OF THE
EVIL UNION. BUT IN A NEIGHBOURING
STAR SYSTEM ANOTHER UNION IS
CAUSING PROBLEMS FOR OUR
CHALLENGED HEROINE.

JAFFA THE TRUMP, DESPOTIC SPACE
GANGSTER AND SATSUMA-SKINNED SLUG,
HAS EMPLOYED THE SERVICES OF
INTERGALACTIC PERSON OF INTEREST
AND BOUNTY HUNTER BOBA FARAGE WHO
IS MYSTERIOUSLY CROPPING UP ALL
OVER THE GALAXY ON AN APPARENT
NON-STOP JOLLY AND STIRRING UP ALL
KINDS OF RUMOURS AND TITTLE-TATTLE.
MAYA MUST DECIDE WHETHER TO SEND
OUT PROBE DROIDS TO PUT A STOP TO
BIG-MOUTHED BOBA ONCE AND FOR ALL
OR TO WOO JAFFA THE TRUMP ON HIS
STATE VISIT BY WEARING A METAL BIKINI.

FACE FACTS

THE TRUTH WILL SET YOU FREE.

SUPERMAN ISN'T COMING TO SAVE US.

FEELING BETTER NOW?

DESIGN FOR LIFE

IMAGINE YOU'RE A TOP FASHION
DESIGNER. DESIGN A GARMENT TO
HELP FUEL YOUR POSITIVITY AND
LIFT YOUR SPIRITS.

THE ONESIE OF PROFOUND COMFORT

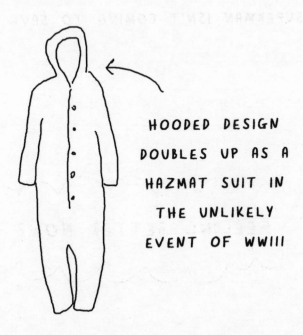

HOODED DESIGN
DOUBLES UP AS A
HAZMAT SUIT IN
THE UNLIKELY
EVENT OF WWIII

PHILOSOPHY RING

CLEAR YOUR HEAD AND REFLECT ON
WHAT YOU ARE LEAVING BEHIND AS
YOU CALMLY BOB ACROSS THE
CHANNEL TO FRANCE.

CORBYN CONFESSION CORNER

CONFESS YOUR SINS AND PURGE YOUR SOUL.

TOUCH YOUR YOUTH

RE-ENERGISE YOURSELF BY
CONNECTING WITH YOUNGER
PEOPLE. GO TO A ROCK FESTIVAL.

THIS
SCEPTIC
ISLE

LEAVE ☐   REMAIN ☐

?

FIND YOUR

SILVER LININGS

BRITAIN'S BROKEN BUT...

... AT LEAST WE STILL HAVE THE
GREAT BRITISH BAKE OFF
(JUST ABOUT).

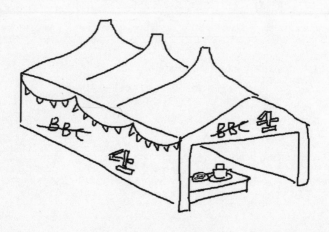

DISTRACTION ACTIONS

DISTRACT YOURSELF FROM YOUR
WORRIES ABOUT THE UK BY
WORRYING ABOUT SOMETHING
MUCH WORSE:

1. WORLD WAR III BREAKS OUT

2. TIME ITSELF ENDS

3. THE SPICE GIRLS RE-FORM

MT -> TM?

"THERE IS NO SUCH
THING AS ∨ ~~SOCIETY~~."
A MAJORITY

USA
HEY GB. BUMPED INTO YOUR OLD PAL NIGEL. NOT SURE I TRUST HIM.
UK
HE'S A . DON'T GET HIM STARTED ON IMMIGRATION .
USA
I SEEN HIM TALKING TO THAT VLAD GUY. THINK THEY'VE GOT SOMETHING GOING ON.
UK
THOUGHT VLAD WAS YOUR MATE?
USA
WAS!! HE TRIED TO RUN MY LIFE. NOBODY TELLS ME WHAT TO DO.
UK
TRU DAT.

BALATORY

GET AWAY FROM BRITISH POLITICS
AND WATCH SOME TV WITH THE KIDS.

JC NUGGETS

WITH JEREMY'S SECOND COMING HE
SEEMS TO HAVE MORE WISDOM THAN
EVER. RECEIVE HIS NUGGETS AND
FEED OFF THEM.

THE SECRET TO
HAPPINESS IS A HEALTHY
BODY AND SOUL

THE SECRET TO A
GOOD SOUFFLE IS
UNINTERRUPTED COOKING

GRIME IS A GENRE OF
MUSIC FUSING UK
GARAGE AND JUNGLE
WITH INFLUENCES FROM
DANCEHALL, HIPPITY-HOP
AND RAGGA.

PROCRASTINATION
STATION

DON'T GET STUCK AT A RED LIGHT
AND BE PROACTIVE.

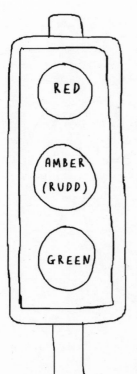

STOP!
YOU MAY BE STUCK HERE
FOR A WHILE...

WAIT WAIT WAIT!
BE PLOTTING AND WHEN IT
IS THE RIGHT TIME POUNCE
AND TAKE CONTROL.

GO(VE) FOR IT!
SAY WHATEVER YOU NEED
TO SAY TO ACHIEVE YOUR
GOALS.

RETENTIVE RELEASE

EMBRACE YOUR INNER PEDANT BY
PULLING ALL THE HAIR OFF THIS
BAR OF SOAP.

CUT AND PASTE

USE THIS SPACE TO DRAW
WHAT YOU HATE ABOUT
LIVING IN BRITAIN.

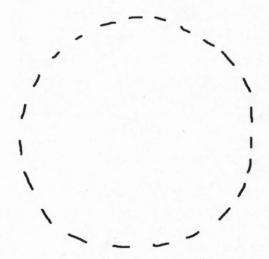

NOW CUT IT OUT, PASTE IT TO A
WALL AND USE IT AS A DARTBOARD.

THERESA MAY'S

CARPENTRY CORNER

A STRONG AND STABLE BABY'S CRADLE.

DON'T
PANIC!

LAUGHTER THERAPY

IT'S FUNNY OLD BOJO THE CLOWN.
WHAT'S HE DOING NOW?

IS HE SLIPPING UP OVER A
DIPLOMATIC BANANA SKIN AGAIN?

REMOVE THE ROT

YOU ARE THE DENTIST OF YOUR OWN
DESTINY. USING THE DRILL OF
CONFIDENCE, REMOVE THE TEETH THAT
ARE CAUSING THE MOST PAIN BEFORE
THE ANAESTHETIC WEARS OFF.

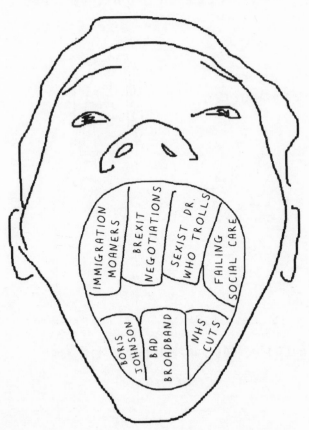

HAMMOND HOUSE
OF HORROR

TO BE AFRAID HELPS US TO
FACE UP TO THE HARD
KNOCKS LIFE THROWS AT US.

INTRODUCING:

THE SHADOW CABINET OF DR
CORBYNARI

BRITAIN IN PIECES

PUT BRITAIN BACK TOGETHER AGAIN.

OH NO. WE APPEAR TO HAVE
LOST SCOTLAND.

THERESA MAY SCHOOL

OF MOTORING

PUT YOURSELF IN LIFE'S
DRIVING SEAT.

RAISE NATIONAL INSURANCE
CONTRIBUTIONS FOR
SELF-EMPLOYED PEOPLE, THEN
PERFORM THIS MANOEUVRE:

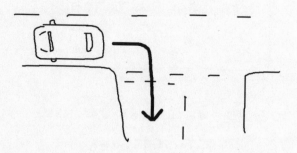

REVERSE AROUND A CORNER

REASONS TO BE
CHEERFUL:

- SPRINGWATCH

- NOEL EDMONDS

- LINDA LUSARDI

- MINT HUMBUGS

- DIY SOS

- QUEEN (THE ROCK GROUP)

- COFFEE WITH CHICORY

- THE SINCLAIR C5

- ANIMAL CLONING

- SLADE

THE BREXIT CAFE

EAT YOURSELF HEALTHY.

2. LUNCH

YOUR BILL

CHEDDAR
1 X ~~BRIE~~ & HAM SANDWICH

CHIPS
1 X ~~FRENCH FRIES~~

IRON BRU
1 X GLASS OF ~~PINOT NOIR~~

TOTAL COST: £66 BILLION

LIFE CHOICES

KEEP CALM...

CADBURY TO CHANGE CHOCOLATE RECIPE FOR CREME EGGS

... AND STOP WHINING

FAKE NEWS

FED UP WITH DEPRESSING HEADLINES?
WHY NOT MAKE UP SOME FAKE ONES
TO CHEER YOURSELF UP?

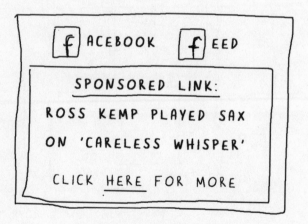

ZONAL HAPPINESS

CREATE SAFE SPACES AROUND YOUR
HOME WHERE YOU CAN BE FREE
FROM STRESS AND ANXIETY.

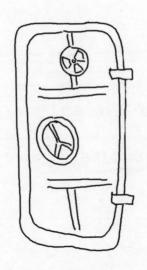

TURN YOUR BASEMENT INTO A BOMB
SHELTER FOR WHEN NORTH KOREA
FIRES A MISSILE THAT ACTUALLY WORKS.

STIFF UPPER LIP

KEEP CALM AND CARRY ON -
TEST YOUR ANGER CONTROL
WITH THIS IMAGE.

ZONAL HAPPINESS

CREATE SAFE SPACES AROUND YOUR
HOME WHERE YOU CAN BE FREE FROM
STRESS AND ANXIETY.

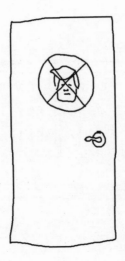

TURN YOUR DOWNSTAIRS LOO
INTO A NO-TRUMPS TOILET.

WHERE'S VLAD?

TEST YOUR POWERS OF OBSERVATION.

ANSWER - HE'S BEHIND THE
SCENES DIRECTING THE SHOW.

THERESA MEH

TAKE A MORE CAREFREE APPROACH
TO LIFE.

EUROSTAR WARS

EPISODE VI - THE RETURN

OF THE REDI

ESCAPE INTO AN EXCITING WORLD OF SCI-FI ADVENTURE. READ THE FOLLOWING PLOT SET-UP AND THEN WRITE AN ENDING.

IN A GALAXY FAR, FAR AWAY, ONE OF THE LAST FEW REDI MASTERS, JEREMI-WAN CORBYNOBI, IS TRYING TO CONVINCE A DISBELIEVING PUBLIC THAT THE ONCE-POWERFUL REDI KNIGHTS ARE STILL RELEVANT. THE REDI BELIEVED IN AN ARCHAIC, UTOPIAN IDEA OF EQUALITY AND SHARED WEALTH, BUT WHEN REDI MASTER DARTH BLAIR TURNED TO THE DARK SIDE AND DESTROYED THE CENTURIES-OLD BELIEF SYSTEM, THE REDI STRUGGLED FOR ACCEPTANCE IN THE GALAXY.

THEN, FROM THE SHADOWS OF THE
GALACTIC BACKBENCHES, STEPPED THE
SILVER-HAIRED, ALMOST GERIATRIC REDI
MASTER, CORBYNOBI. AT FIRST
PRESENTING AS A BEFUDDLED AND
FRANKLY WISHY-WASHY LEADER,
CORBYNOBI SECURED A STUNNING
TURNAROUND BY ACTUALLY CARING
ABOUT ISSUES AND PEOPLE.
THIS, AS WELL AS HANGING
OUT WITH YOUNGSTERS AND
PRETENDING TO LISTEN TO
THEIR MUSIC, SUDDENLY MADE
THE REDI COOL AGAIN.
BUT CORBYNOBI DIDN'T
ACTUALLY WIN ANYTHING.
UNTIL...

BRITAIN'S NEXT TOP
PRIME MINISTER

DISILLUSIONED WITH THE UK'S
CURRENT LEADERSHIP? WHY NOT
IMAGINE SOMEONE BETTER AS PM?

CAPTAIN
MAINWARING

ANNE DIAMOND

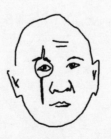

BLOFELD

BRAINERCISE

GIVE YOURSELF A MENTAL WORKOUT
WITH THIS BRITISH WORDSEARCH.

B	O	R	I	S	V	D	N	H	S	M
O	F	J	G	H	Q	A	K	C	V	A
V	S	L	T	E	A	M	J	A	N	Y
R	R	Y	S	U	L	N	A	S	G	X
I	F	G	O	B	A	A	G	O	V	E
L	C	U	R	R	Y	T	H	E	W	F
H	F	S	R	M	O	I	O	K	S	E
U	K	P	Y	T	R	O	T	P	S	O
J	E	R	E	M	Y	N	I	I	Y	P
O	O	O	Y	G	S	H	A	U	E	K
F	Q	U	T	D	C	L	G	D	F	G
M	C	T	W	I	A	D	H	W	D	F
R	T	N	E	M	A	I	L	R	A	P

NHS	BORIS	JEREMY
MAY	CURRY	SPROUT
ROT	SORRY	MALAISE
CHIPS	ROYAL	DAMNATION
GOVE	BOVRIL	PARLIAMENT

FACE FACTS

THE TRUTH WILL SET YOU FREE.

WE REALLY ARE LEAVING THE EU.
TRUMP REALLY DID GET ELECTED.
WAGON WHEELS REALLY ARE
SLIGHTLY SMALLER.

FEELING BETTER NOW?

DESIGN FOR LIFE

IMAGINE YOU'RE A TOP FASHION
DESIGNER. DESIGN A GARMENT TO
HELP FUEL YOUR POSITIVITY AND
LIFT YOUR SPIRITS.

THE SARONG OF ULTIMATE SERENITY

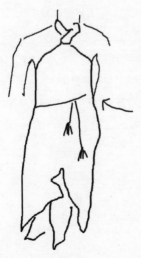

TASSELLED BELT CAN
BE TIGHTENED IN
TIMES OF AUSTERITY

POSITIVITY PAIRING

FORGET HOW MISERABLE YOU ARE BY
TRYING TO RE-UNITE THESE POPULAR
BRITISH PAIRINGS.

ROD HULL
AND
RONNIE BARKER

LITTLE
AND
PHILIP HAMMOND

KEITH HARRIS
AND
GREAVSIE

TONY BLAIR
AND
CANNON

LARGE
AND
BALL

MATTHEW CORBETT
AND
RONNIE CORBETT

THERESA MAY
AND
SOOTY

SAINT
AND
PACE

HALE
AND
GORDON BROWN

ORVILLE
AND
EMU

CORBYN CONFESSION
CORNER

CONFESS YOUR SINS AND PURGE
YOUR SOUL.

TOUCH YOUR YOUTH

RE-ENERGISE YOURSELF BY
CONNECTING WITH YOUNGER PEOPLE.
WHY NOT MAKE UP A RAP SONG?

I MAY BE OLD BUT I'M A SO SOLID
GEEZER. I DON'T SMOKE WEED BUT I
LOVE A MALTESER.

JC-MC! JC-MC!

DVD DETOX

ESCAPE THE HARSH REALITIES OF BRITISH POLITICS BY RELAXING IN FRONT OF YOUR FAVOURITE DVD.

THE FANTASTIC MR LIAM FOX.

WHERE ANGELA EAGLES DARE.

SALMOND FISHING IN THE YEMEN.

ME BEFORE EU.

FARAGE – INTERNATIONAL PERSON OF INTEREST

TRY TO BE OPEN-MINDED AND TAKE OTHERS' INTERESTS INTO ACCOUNT.

BLAH, BLAH, BLAH. WHAT DO YOU MEAN, YOU DON'T DRINK?! YOU BIG WUSS! COME ON – DOWN IN ONE. BLAH, BLAH, BLAH...

DISTRACTION ACTIONS

DISTRACT YOURSELF FROM YOUR
WORRIES ABOUT THE UK BY
WORRYING ABOUT SOMETHING
MUCH WORSE:

1. WE ENTER A NEW ICE AGE

2. ALIENS INVADE AND MAKE US
   THEIR SLAVES

3. THEY STOP MAKING HOBNOBS

MT -> TM?

"THE LADY'S ~~NOT~~ FOR TURNING."

JC NUGGETS

WITH JEREMY'S SECOND COMING HE
SEEMS TO HAVE MORE WISDOM THAN
EVER. RECEIVE HIS NUGGETS AND
FEED OFF THEM.

ALL LIVING CREATURES
ARE EQUALLY IMPORTANT

CARY GRANT USED LSD IN
HIS SIXTIES TO TREAT
AN IDENTITY CRISIS

GRIME MC JME'S
REAL NAME IS
JAMIE ADENUGA

DOLPHIN GYMKHANA

YOU ARE A MAGICAL SILVER DOLPHIN CALLED SUKI. NOW JUMP OVER THE WAVES OF BREXIT OBSTACLES AS YOU MAKE YOUR WAY TO CALAIS.

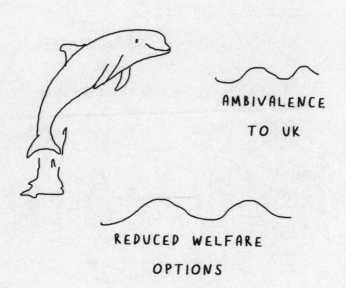

AMBIVALENCE TO UK

REDUCED WELFARE OPTIONS

SWIM, SUKI, SWIM!

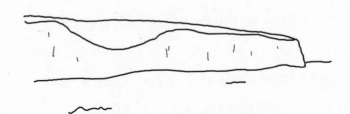

STRUGGLING
UK ECONOMY

RESTRICTED
MIGRATION

LIMITED TRADE
PARTNERS

IT'S HAMMOND TIME!

KEEP WITHIN YOUR BUDGET.

EXTRA RESOURCES FOR THOSE ON THE POVERTY LINE?

POSITIVITY PAN PIPES

IMAGINE YOU'RE A CHEEKY FOREST
FAUN WHO HAS FALLEN FOUL OF THE
WELFARE SYSTEM. YOU'RE TRAPPED IN
SOCIAL HOUSING, DEPENDENT ON
WELFARE AND ADDICTED TO SPICE.

PICK UP YOUR PAN PIPES AND SOFTLY
BLOW ALL NEGATIVITY AWAY.

RETENTIVE RELEASE

EMBRACE YOUR INNER PEDANT BY
PUTTING THE LIDS BACK ON
THESE JARS PROPERLY.

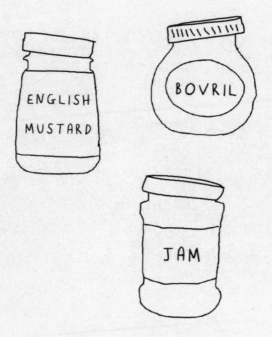

RED, WHITE AND BLUE
TINTED SPECTACLES

WHY NOT CONTRAST THE
HOPELESSNESS OF REALITY AGAINST
RECENT GB GLORIES.

FAILING NHS ——— LONDON 2012

RISING WAVES OF ____ LONDON 2012
RACISM PARALYMPICS

CRUMBLING ____ ER... LONDON
EDUCATION SYSTEM OLYMPICS

COLLAPSING ____ UM...
CURRENCY LONDON?

THERESA MAY'S
CARPENTRY CORNER

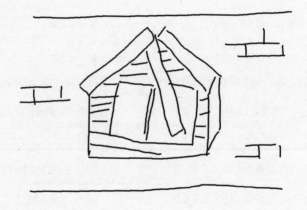

A STRONG AND STABLE GABLE.

MORE
RAIN,
VICAR?

LAUGHTER THERAPY

LOOK - HERE'S FUNNY OLD BOJO THE
CLOWN. WHAT'S HE UP TO?

IS HE JUGGLING WITH YOUR
FUTURE AGAIN?

LEARN TO BE
PATRIOTIC AGAIN

HAVE A GOOD OLD SING-SONG
AROUND THE OLD JOANNA.

'PACK UP YOUR TROUBLES IN
YOUR OLD KIT BAG AND
SMILE, SMILE, SMILE.'

(EVEN IF YOU WANT TO CRY, CRY, CRY
AND MOVE TO NEW ZEALAND.)

HAMMOND HOUSE

OF HORROR

TO BE AFRAID HELPS US TO FACE UP TO THE HARD KNOCKS LIFE THROWS AT US.

NOSFERATHERESA

IDENTITY IDENTIFIER

HELP TO CENTRE YOURSELF. PONDER
WHAT IT IS TO BE YOU –
A STRONG, PROUD BRITISH INDIVIDUAL.

CIRCLE THE WORDS THAT
DESCRIBE YOU:

- WELCOMING
- TOLERANT
- PROUD
- CONTRADICTORY NITWIT
- INTOLERANT TOSSPOT
- OPEN
- HAPPY
- CRAP CROUPIER
- CLINICALLY DEPRESSED
- JINGOISTIC BIGOT
- DELUSIONS OF GRANDEUR

THERESA MAY SCHOOL

OF MOTORING

PUT YOURSELF IN LIFE'S
DRIVING SEAT.

WHEN YOUR INSTRUCTOR TAPS THE
DASHBOARD PERFORM THIS MANOEUVRE:

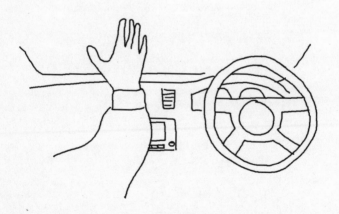

THE EMERGENCY SNAP ELECTION

GREAT BRITS

BRITT EKLAND
BRIT MARLING
BRITNEY SPEARS
BRITA WATER FILTERS

POLITICAL PARTY TIME

IT'S YOUR PARTY. BLUDGEON YOUR
WAY THROUGH PUBLIC OPINION TO
GET WHAT YOU WANT IN A GAME OF
BRITISH BULLDOG.

FIND YOUR
SILVER LININGS

BRITAIN'S BROKEN BUT...

... AT LEAST WE STILL HAVE THE
RECORDINGS OF CHAS & DAVE.

'GERTCHA'

'RABBIT, RABBIT
YAP YAP'

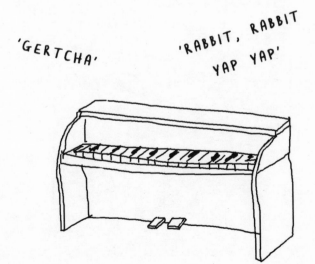

FAKE NEWS

FED UP WITH DEPRESSING HEADLINES?
WHY NOT MAKE UP SOME FAKE ONES
TO CHEER YOURSELF UP?

REASONS TO BE
CHEERFUL

- MICHAEL CAINE

- ICELAND (NOT THE COUNTRY)

- MUSHY PEAS

- LAMBERT AND BUTLER

- UNIVERSITY CHALLENGE

- COLA CUBES

- DAME JUDI DENCH (BUT NOT WHEN SHE'S
  SINGING 'SEND IN THE CLOWNS')

- THE ROBIN RELIANT

- CROSSROADS MOTEL

- JUSTIN FLETCHER

LIFE CHOICES

GET OUT OF BED...

... AND STOP CRYING.

STIFF UPPER LIP

KEEP CALM AND CARRY ON -
TEST YOUR ANGER CONTROL WITH
THIS IMAGE.

THE BREXIT JOB

WHERE'S VLAD?

TEST YOUR POWERS OF
OBSERVATION.

ANSWER - HE'S PULLING THE STRINGS
OF THE WORLD LEADER PUPPET.

THERESA MEH

TAKE A MORE CAREFREE
APPROACH TO LIFE.

BRITAIN'S NEXT TOP
PRIME MINISTER

DISILLUSIONED WITH THE UK'S
CURRENT LEADERSHIP? WHY NOT
IMAGINE SOMEONE BETTER AS PM?

BASIL FAWLTY

KEITH
RICHARDS

THE ALIEN
FROM ALIEN

HOW BRITISH ARE YOU?

TEST THE DEPTH OF YOUR BRITISH
SPIRIT WITH THESE MULTIPLE CHOICE
QUESTIONS, THEN ADD UP YOUR SCORES.

A. WHAT DOES THE WORD 'SORRY' MEAN
TO YOU?

1: IT'S AN APOLOGY

2: IT'S A PASSIVE-AGGRESSIVE ACCUSATION

3: IT'S A 1980'S TV SHOW WITH RONNIE
CORBETT

B. WHAT IS A CHIP?

1: IT'S SOMETHING IN A COMPUTER

2: IT'S SOMETHING YOU EAT WITH FISH

3: IT'S SOMETHING YOU KEEP ON YOUR
SHOULDER

 C. WHAT IS FOOTBALL

1: NFL

2: SOCCER

3: A BUNCH OF OVERPAID PONCES, WHINGEING
ABOUT NOTHING

D. WHAT IS A 'BUGGER'?

1: BOTTY SEX

2: A SPY

3: A DAFT HA'P'ORTH

E. WHAT SIDE OF THE ROAD DO YOU DRIVE?

1: THE RIGHT

2: THE LEFT

3: NEITHER: TOO MANY POTHOLES

F. WHAT IS A 'Q'?

1: THE LETTER AFTER 'P'.

2: BOND'S BOFFIN

3: SOMETHING YOU STAND IN FOR HOURS.

_____

NOW TOT UP YOUR SCORES-

13-18 - CONGRATULATIONS. YOU ARE ABOUT
AS BRITISH AS THEY COME.

7-12 - NOT QUITE AS BRITISH AS YOU COULD
BE. TRY HARDER.

1-6 - BIENVENUE EN GRANDE-BRETAGNE,
PARLEZ-VOUS ANGLAIS?

BRAINERCISE

GIVE YOURSELF A MENTAL WORKOUT
WITH THIS THERESA MAZE.

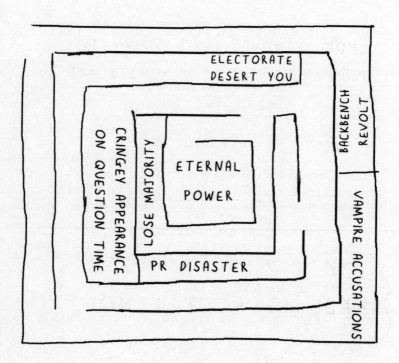

FACE FACTS

THE TRUTH WILL SET YOU FREE.

NOEL EDMONDS ISN'T GOING TO
POP UP AT THE LAST MINUTE AND
SCREAM 'GOTCHA'.

FEELING BETTER NOW?

DESIGN FOR LIFE

IMAGINE YOU'RE A TOP FASHION
DESIGNER. DESIGN A GARMENT TO
HELP FUEL YOUR POSITIVITY AND
LIFT YOUR SPIRITS.

THE TROUSERS OF INFINITE
PROSPERITY

BIG POCKETS FOR
ALL THE EXTRA
MONEY YOU'LL
DEFINITELY NEED
AFTER BREXIT

EAT

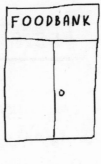

FOODBANK

SHELTER

FULL

SLEEP

RAVE

special brew

REPEAT!!

TEMPTATION TEST

YOU ARE HOLDING A PERFECTLY RIPE
JUICY TOMATO WHEN YOU BUMP INTO
A POLITICIAN YOU REALLY DETEST.
DO YOU:

1 - POLITELY BID GOOD DAY AND GO
ABOUT YOUR BUSINESS.

2 - GREEDILY DEVOUR THE DELICIOUS
FRUIT, REVELLING IN THE
POLITICIAN'S JEALOUS GAZE.

3 - TAKE THREE DEEP BREATHS,
CROSS THE ROAD THEN THROW THE
TOMATO FROM MORE OF A DISTANCE
SO AS TO GET A BETTER 'SPLAT'?

TOUCH YOUR YOUTH

RE-ENERGISE YOURSELF BY CONNECTING WITH YOUNGER PEOPLE.

PHOTOBOMB AS MANY SELFIES
AS YOU CAN.

DVD DETOX

ESCAPE THE HARSH REALITIES
OF BRITISH POLITICS BY
RELAXING IN FRONT OF YOUR
FAVOURITE DVD.

FRIED GREENING TOMATOES AT THE
WHISTLE STOP CAFE

THE HAN-GOVE-ER

A BRIDGE TOO FARAGE

WE NEED TO TALK ABOUT CORBYN

FIND YOUR
SILVER LININGS

BRITAIN'S BROKEN BUT...

... AT LEAST WE STILL HAVE
JAFFA CAKES

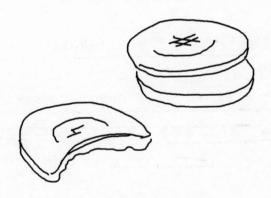

DISTRACTION ACTIONS

DISTRACT YOURSELF FROM YOUR
WORRIES ABOUT THE UK BY
WORRYING ABOUT SOMETHING
MUCH WORSE:

1. GLOBAL WARMING MELTS THE
   ICE CAPS

2. GOD SENDS A PLAGUE OF
   LOCUSTS

3. DOCTOR WHO GETS
   CANCELLED

MT -> TM?

"I DON'T MIND HOW MUCH MY
MINISTERS TALK, AS LONG AS
THEY ~~DO WHAT I SAY~~."
          $\bigvee$

DON'T CONSTANTLY UNDERMINE
MY POLICIES IN A
MACHIAVELLIAN ATTEMPT TO
SEIZE POWER FROM ME.

NATURAL HEALING

IMAGINE THERE IS SUCH A THING AS
A MAGIC MONEY TREE.

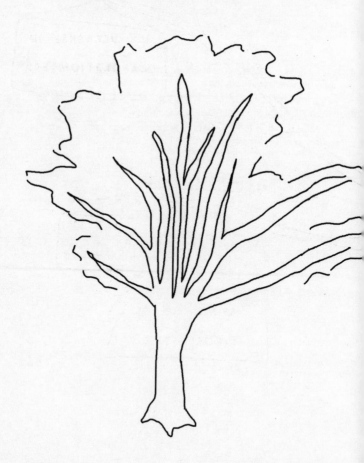

WRITE YOUR FISCAL WISHES DOWN
AND HANG THEM FROM A BRANCH OF
THE TREE.

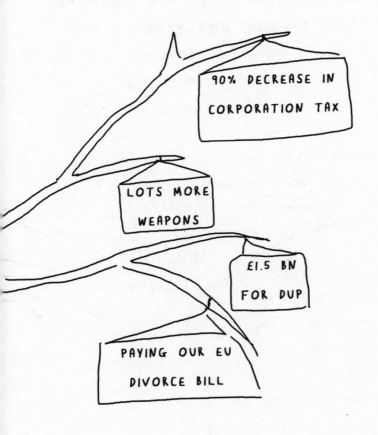

JC NUGGETS

WITH JEREMY'S SECOND COMING HE
SEEMS TO HAVE MORE WISDOM THAN
EVER. RECEIVE HIS NUGGETS AND
FEED OFF THEM.

PEARLS OF WISDOM
CAN SOMETIMES BE
IRONIC WHEN USED
SARCASTICALLY

POPULAR TV DETECTIVE,
EDDIE SHOESTRING, WAS
PLAYED BY ACTOR
TREVOR EVE

FROM 2013 ONWARDS
GRIME PRODUCERS
CREATED 'INSTRUMENTAL
GRIME' AND COMPETED
IN 'WAR DUBS', MUCH
LIKE THE BREAKDANCE
BATTLES OF THE 1980'S

FR
HAHAHA - YOU KNACKERED YOURSELF WITH YOUR GENERAL ELECTION.
UK
SHUT UP FRANCE. IT WASN'T ALL MY FAULT.
FR
ANYWAY, I'M NOT TALKING TO YOU ANYMORE. HANGING OUT WITH DE NOW. MUCH MORE FUN. DE'S GOT MUCH BETTER CARS THAN YOU.
UK
DON'T CARE. MUCH HAPPIER ON MY OWN ANYWAY. I DON'T NEED YOU. I DON'T NEED ANYONE!
FRANCE?
FRANCE ARE YOU THERE?!

POSITIVE MENTAL
ATTITUDE

TRY TO HAVE A P.M.A. EVEN IF
YOUR WHOLE WORLD IS IN
TURMOIL.

P.M. MAY

RETENTIVE RELEASE

EMBRACE YOUR INNER PEDANT BY
REARRANGING THE CONTENTS OF
THIS BADLY FILLED DISHWASHER.

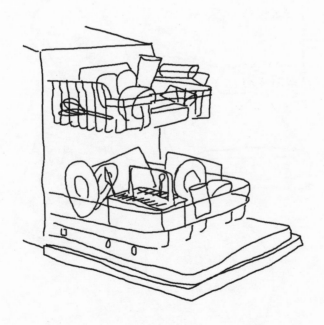

CONVERSATION
CONVERTER

REPLACE DEPRESSING
POLITICAL DISCOURSE AT
WORK WITH BISCUIT BANTER.
DISCUSS...

THERESA MAY'S
CARPENTRY CORNER

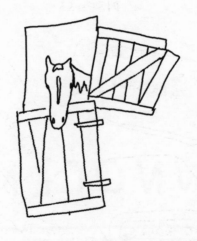

A STRONG AND STABLE STABLE.

DAVID DAVIS

IS

INNOCENT

LAUGHTER THERAPY

HERE COMES BOJO THE CLOWN.
WHAT'S HE DOING THIS TIME?

IS HIS INTEGRITY HANGING
BY A THREAD AGAIN?

REMOVE THE ROT

YOU ARE THE SURGEON OF
SERENITY. USING YOUR SCALPEL OF
CALM, REMOVE THE ORGANS THAT
ARE SPREADING ROT, WITHOUT
KILLING THE PATIENT.

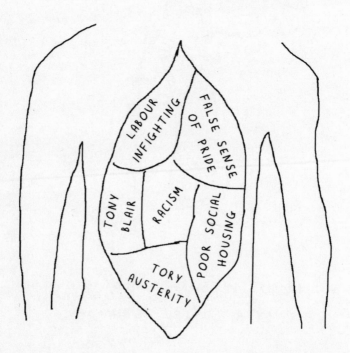

HAMMOND HOUSE

OF HORROR

 TO BE AFRAID HELPS US TO FACE UP TO THE HARD KNOCKS LIFE THROWS AT US.

INTRODUCING:

BOJO THE SCARY CLOWN

JINGO BINGO

CREATE YOUR OWN JINGOISTIC BINGO LINGO. HERE ARE SOME TO GET YOU STARTED.

(23)	SCOTCH EGG REVIVAL
(8)	DIRTY AUNTY DOREEN
(100)	CHURCHILL'S NAPSACK
(10)	LINDA'S STOCKINGS
(77)	LAST ORDERS
(41)	CHEGWIN'S CRACKERS
(32)	LESBIAN PICCALILLI

THERESA MAY SCHOOL

OF MOTORING

PUT YOURSELF IN LIFE'S
DRIVING SEAT.

IT'S NOT TOO LATE TO TURN
THIS CAR CRASH AROUND!

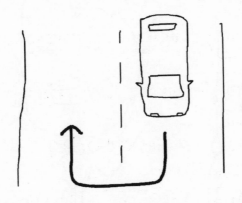

THE EU-TURN

POLITICAL PARTY TIME

IT'S YOUR PARTY. SEE IF YOU CAN
PIN THE TAIL ON BORIS JOHNSON.

THE BREXIT CAFE

EAT YOURSELF HEALTHY.

3. DINNER

STARTERS

~~ITALIAN GNOCCHI~~

BIRDS EYE
POTATO WAFFLES

MAINS

~~SPANISH OMELETTE~~

FINDUS CRISPY
PANCAKES

DESSERT

ETON MESS

FAKE NEWS

FED UP WITH DEPRESSING HEADLINES?
WHY NOT MAKE UP SOME FAKE ONES
TO CHEER YOURSELF UP?

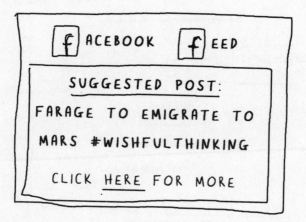

LIFE CHOICES

PULL YOUR SOCKS UP...

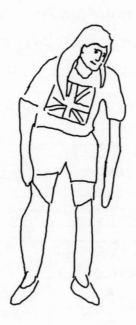

... AND GET ON WITH IT!

STIFF UPPER LIP

KEEP CALM AND CARRY ON -
TEST YOUR ANGER CONTROL
WITH THIS IMAGE.

NEW

BALLS,

PLEASE

ZONAL HAPPINESS

CREATE SAFE SPACES AROUND YOUR HOME WHERE YOU CAN BE FREE FROM STRESS AND ANXIETY.

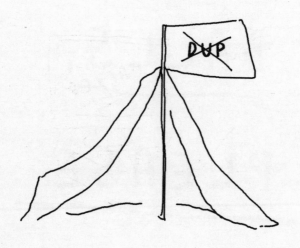

TURN YOUR DUVET INTO A DUP-FREE TEEPEE.

WHERE'S VLAD?

TEST YOUR POWERS OF
OBSERVATION.

ANSWER - HE'S INSIDE YOUR
COMPUTER.

CAPRICIOUS WHIM

THROW CAUTION TO THE WIND AND
BE NAUGHTY!

RUN THROUGH A FIELD OF
WHEAT IF YOU DARE!

WHATEVER NEXT?

CREATIVE SOLUTIONS

FEELING HOPELESSLY TRAPPED ON THIS LONELY ISLAND? WHY NOT WRITE A RESCUE MESSAGE, PUT IT IN A BOTTLE AND THROW IT OUT TO SEA?

NO ONE WILL EVER READ IT, BUT IT'LL BE A NICE DAY OUT. YOU COULD HAVE A CORNETTO.

CONVERSATION

CONVERTER

REPLACE DEPRESSING POLITICAL
DISCOURSE AT WORK WITH A
CONFECTIONERY CONFERENCE.
DISCUSS...

DESIGN YOUR OWN
PERFECT PRIME MINISTER

BE CREATIVE. BUILD A NEW
P.M. OUT OF OLD ONES.

HAROLD
MACMILLAN'S
MOUSTACHE

HAROLD
WILSON'S PIPE

WINSTON
CHURCHILL'S BELLY

JOHN MAJOR'S
VOICEBOX

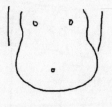

TONY BLAIR'S
DEMON EYES

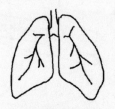

MARGARET
THATCHER'S IRON
LUNGS

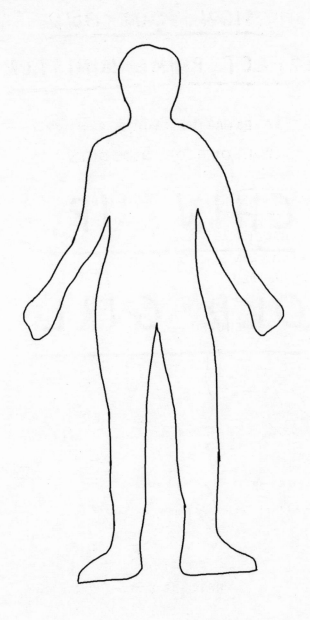

CHIN UP,

OLD GIRL